Laure

by David Martz
illustrated by Elizabeth Allen

HOUGHTON MIFFLIN HARCOURT
School Publishers

Printed in China

ISBN-13: 978-0-547-01784-6
ISBN-10: 0-547-01784-7

10 11 12 13 0940 18 17 16 15 14 13
4500443494

When Lauren Otter's shell phone rang in her office on Monday morning, she wasn't working like a good lawyer should be. Instead, Lauren was swimming in her office pool. That was way more fun than work! And fun was what sea otters loved more than anything.

Lauren kept swimming, and the phone kept ringing. Finally, she climbed out of the pool.

"Oh, well. I guess even otter lawyers have to work sometime," she said. She flipped open the phone and put it next to her tiny, fur-covered ear.

"You have reached the law offices of Lauren Otter, legal eagle," she said. "If you have been in an accident or were the victim—"

A scared voice on the other end of the line interrupted her. It was her friend, Sammy Seal.

"Lauren, I need your help right away!" Sammy said. "I'm in the Rocky Beach Jail, and they won't let me go."

Lauren just giggled. She thought that Sammy must be joking. Sammy was the most honest sea creature she knew. He would never break the law.

"This is no laughing matter, Lauren," he said. "The police arrested me this morning. They say I stole 100 clams from the Grand Bank!"

Sammy worked at the Grand Bank. He was very serious about his job. Suddenly, Lauren realized Sammy wasn't joking.

"I'll be right there, Sammy," said Lauren.

At the Rocky Beach Jail, Sammy told Lauren what had happened. Lauren tried to pay attention to her new client, but she kept thinking about how much fun it would be to swing from the bars of the jail.

"A bank customer gave me 100 clams to save for him," Sammy said. "At the end of the day, I put the clams in the safe, just the way I always do."

Lauren took notes, but she was still thinking of swinging on those bars.

"But Mr. Shark in the loan department said I stole the clams," Sammy went on. "The police are convinced it's true. They say that they even have photos to prove it!"

"Don't worry, Sammy," Lauren Otter said. "Photos can't prove you're guilty if you didn't take the clams. There's something fishy about that Mr. Shark, and I'm going to find out what it is."

Sammy felt better—but only a little.

Lauren Otter was now swinging on the jail bars.

The next morning, all the sea animals gathered for Sammy Seal's trial. When Judge Walrus sat down, everyone was still and quiet—except Lauren Otter.

"Woo-hoo!" she shouted, sliding across one of the court benches.

"Lauren Otter, come to order!" shouted Judge Walrus.

Lauren returned to her seat.

The trial began when Mr. Shark sat in the witness stand. Mr. Shark told his side of the story. The jury listened carefully. But not Lauren Otter.

"Look what I can do!" Lauren shouted. She balanced a law book on her nose.

"Lauren Otter! Come to order!" shouted Judge Walrus.

Lauren returned to her seat.

Then Mr. Shark showed the jury the photos taken by the bank cameras.

"As you can see," Mr. Shark said. "These photos show Sammy Seal taking the 100 clams."

A murmur went through the crowd.

Next, it was Lauren Otter's turn to talk. But Lauren was doing something else. She was juggling three members of the jury!

"Lauren Otter, come to order!" Judge Walrus yelled again.

Lauren tried to pay attention. She called Sammy Seal to the witness stand.

"I put the 100 clams in the safe, just as I always do," Sammy told the jury.

"A likely story!" shouted Mr. Shark from his seat.

Lauren Otter looked at Mr. Shark. That's when she noticed a strange bulge in his jacket.

"Now, what could that be?" she wondered.

Lauren climbed up onto the judge's desk.

"Lauren Otter, come to order!" shouted Judge Walrus one more time.

Instead of coming to order, Lauren did a back flip. "Hey Sharkey, let's see you try that!"

"I am not here to—" Mr. Shark began.

"Are you too chicken?" Lauren asked with a smirk.

Sharks do not like being called chicken. Mr. Shark jumped up on the judge's desk, turned, and did a flip. It was not as good as Lauren's flip, but…

Suddenly, 100 clams clattered from the shark's jacket and rolled across the floor!

"Ah-ha!" shouted Lauren Otter as she pointed at Mr. Shark. "I knew it!"

"Mr. Shark took the clams and blamed me!" Sammy Seal shouted.

As the police led Mr. Shark away, everyone began to cheer. Lauren Otter had saved the day! But Lauren didn't care. She was busy practicing her back flip.

Responding

TARGET SKILL **Conclusions** Copy the chart below. Fill in three story details that show that Lauren Otter has trouble paying attention to her work.

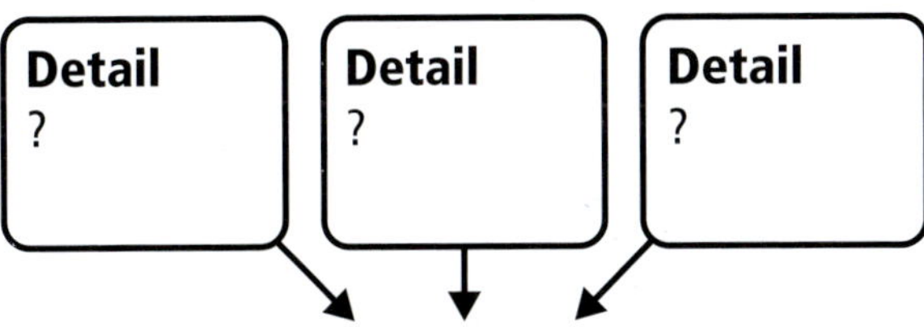

Conclusion Lauren Otter has trouble paying attention to her work.

Write About It

Text to Text Think of another story you know with a character who has fun while working. Do you think it is possible to do a good job and have fun, too? Write a paragraph that gives your opinion about this. Include examples from the stories you have read to support your opinion.

convinced	murmur
guilty	pointed
honest	stand
jury	trial

TARGET SKILL **Conclusions** Use details to figure out ideas that the author doesn't state.

TARGET STRATEGY **Infer/Predict** Use clues to figure out more about the selection.

GENRE A **fantasy** is a story that could not happen in real life.